A Bizarre Sentence
by Trisha Georgiou

Reviews

Trisha Georgiou confronts and deploys the conundrums of the English language in her excellent volume *A Bizarre Sentence*. Not content with using anaphora (repeating an initial phrase over and over), she takes the words "bizarre sentence" and repeats them throughout the volume. Her tool is polysemy and it is also often her subject. Polysemy is the coexistence of many meanings in a single word or words. She masterfully brings this to the apex in her poem Confusion, in English. She creates distinct sentences with "will will will will" and "police police police." Bizarre sentences, indeed. Again, not content with repeating words for singular effect, the words are also alive as sentences. The word "bizarre" bends in her volume. Sometimes it means simply strange, but often it connotes a feeling of helplessness. As she writes in the poem In Limbo: "so much of this bizarre sentence/ is out of our control." Often we are compelled to come to terms with the many meanings of "sentence." Of course it is jail term or grammatical unit. But it can also be both. Her multi-lingual poem In Unison is a prayer for world peace in many languages. She even links the word to DNA sequences in Energy Works. Georgiou consciously works in both the political and person realms: from the 9/11 attacks in Towers Falling to having a child in Pregnancy. Sometimes she works in both as in overheard conversations about a gay dad in Cafe Conversations. When non-native English speakers begin to learn the language, they may be challenged by the many meanings of the words. Georgiou may lament the bizarre sentences as well, but she also revels in their mystery.

— Shea Doyle, poet & playwright

As we flip the page in Trisha Georgiou's book, *A Bizarre Sentence,* she layers bizarreness, one moment on top of another, cements them into a solid structure that shows the bizarre facets of life we live.

—Salvatore Marici, author of *Mortals, Natures, and Their Spirits* and *Swish, Swirl & Sniff*

Trisha Georgiou's " A Bizarre Sentence" takes word-play on a journey through truth, absurdity, love and whimsy. Try to read "Confusion in English" without developing an immediate desire to add a stanza or two! A very enjoyable and thought-provoking read, highly recommended.

—Wayne Sapp, author of *Dinky Dau* and *Arctic Lions*

© 2015 Trisha Georgiou

All rights reserved

ISBN 978-0-9851944-7-5

918 studio press

Published by 918*studio* press

www.918studio.net

Davenport, IA

Formatting and design by Sliced Moon Designs
www.slicedmoondesigns.com

Cover photograph by Ciarán O'Sullivan, Cork, Ireland

Also by Trisha Georgiou

My Name is A

Quartered Enlightenment

A New Life and other poems of Living Passion

For my three shining stars.
Thank you for living a writer's life with me

and for Ciarán.

A Bizarre Sentence
Trisha Georgiou

Table of Contents

Cafe Conversations	1
Songwriter	2
In Unison	3
A Rubbled View	4
Confusion in English	6
Energy Works	7
Untitled	8
Pregnancy	9
Towers Falling	10
In Ferguson	12
Holidaze	13
Vampires Vacuuming	14

Twitterpated	16
Anxiety	17
Door Mats	18
Food	20
Cancer	21
Church Control	22
Gross Anatomy	24
In Limbo	26
Killing Game	27
Political Sentences	28
Writing Glasses	30
Free as the Whirligigs	32

Cafe Conversations

My husband, Bob, said to the kids and I
    during dinner last night, I am gay.
Johnny failed math again,
    but Amy was voted prom queen.
To increase your return by thirty percent, invest all
    of your savings with me.
She died yesterday. Do you want more coffee?
I just couldn't decide between the blue Kate Spade or the
        Louis Vuitton,
    so I bought them both.
How do you apply for food stamps?
I'm such a wreck, my daughter won't pick a major at
        Yale.
Those goddamn democrats with Obama Care, ruining
        our country.
Happy Birthday, dear friend.
Holy Crap! Really?
Hey, I caught you, hiding in the corner writing.
        How's it goin'?
I have a few bizarre sentences.

Songwriter

Piano keys dusted.
Banjo strings tuned.
strike, pick, play
to find perfect notes
for musical phrases.

Songs to sing
from poems written
keys major, minor
melody, harmony.

Chords, arpeggios
bizarre sentences
come together,
songwriter.

In Unison

ادعي ان يعم السلام في الارض
Dünya barışı için Dua ediyorum.
Ich bete um Weltfrieden
May dunya may aman kay liye duaago hon
Sto pregando per pace in tutto il
προσεύχονται για την παγκόσμια ειρήνη
proséfchontai gia tin pankósmia eiríni
Je prie pour la paix dans le monde entier
I am praying for world peace
من برای صلح جهانی دعا میکنم

A Rubbled View

Thousands upon thousands
traverse these glass doors,
traveled painted yellow stairs
to fill all seats, galore.

Teams, fans, excitement, cheers,
pure energy contained in concrete bowl.
Over a decade my work
soaked in the plaster walls.

Until today, the crane came,
I turned off the Pairc's lights.
Destruction intently began.
Rubble, dust, blocked view.

One last time, light peered through
illuminating my gaze, pictures captured,
ingrained living memories
while sounds of demolition, deafening.

I stood there frozen in grit, debris
watching, listening
my work, memories, collapsing,
a bizarre sentence, state of being.

Gathering a few bricks, fallen pieces
history for Irish souls,
to carry the past forward
into the new stadium.

Confusion, in English

Buffalo Buffalo buffalo
Bison (from) Buffalo trick
Buffalo Buffalo
(another) bison from Buffalo.

Ship shipping ship ship,
A boat-shipping boat transports
ship shipping ship
(a) boat-shipping boat.

Will will will will.
If it is it, it is it.
Police police police.
Ugg, the lexical ambiguity.

Nouns, verbs, parts of speech
compound participle adjectives
Yikes, English is confusing, bizarre
amazing any sentences are written.

Energy Works

Imagine, the essence
of how you are made,
electrons, protons,
cells, charges vibrating.

DNA, ribosomal nucleotides
inherited traits, emotional states,
patterns, past lives from ancestors,
guilt, sorrow, toxins, pushed deep inside

places we have yet to discover, but feel
walls keeping us from our dreams, achieving.
How can you love when there are blocks you can't see?
Stuff you didn't know existed, sadness, grief clouding.

Now, imagine letting it all go. Propensities for illness,
addictions, mental disturbances. Awareness is healing.
Your mind can choose to change bizarre DNA coding
sentences with light, music, color, exhaling.

words stir spirit mind
living evokes emotion
a bizarre sentence

Pregnancy

What started as two cells
smaller than a pin's head,
is now eight pounds and counting.
I have greatly expanded.

Why do women enjoy this?
I'm constantly sick.
A beached whale has nothing
on me, when I sit.

Hormone surges, weird cravings,
how much pickle juice did I drink?
Ice cream, hot sauce, olives galore,
no one asked why, but they gave me more.

My body was taken over
by this growing alien inside.
Terror, fear, engulfs my thoughts,
the process of getting this creature out.

Pregnancy, the bizarrest forty week sentence
of course, mine lasted forty-three,
until all of it was over
when I held and snuggled, the baby.

Towers Are Falling Down

On a sofa in rural Illinois, the sun shines
through my window, harmony and peace
as I nurse my baby. A news report
interrupted my PBS gardening documentary.

A tower fell, the second just hit.
terrorism on American soil
I just couldn't grasp that
bizarre sentence.

Turning the channel to CNN,
watching the destruction over and over again.
Fear, terror, my mind locked unable to register.
Was this reality, not an action flick?

My heart stopped, my friend in New York,
the call did go through, as she watched debris
flying past her fifteenth story window,
voice shaking with fear, terror, I love you.

Both towers fell, the Pentagon hit
death toll kept rising in the rubbish,
thousands perished. I had to go.
I wanted to serve, make a difference.

The magnitude never fully processed
until falling to my knees at Ground Zero.
In the midst of despair, strangers unite
all suffering, all working together through fright.

Whatever the cause, your beliefs, terrorism,
theory of conspiracy,
the business of war needed funding,
half way down the poll,
the American flag still waves.

In Ferguson

Trying to make sense of this bizarre sentence
we call, life on Earth.
Humans fighting because of what?
Colors of skin, money, authority, attitude,
violence in the name of righteousness,
doesn't it bring more pain, hatred to the streets?
Our black brother, Rev. Martin Luther King Jr.
to all of the people, preached love and peace.
I can't judge or understand these unsettled souls
because of the color of my skin, life.
Burning businesses, destroying your neighbors
Can this be right, just?
This bizarre state of mind, sentence, riots,
words of peace must be written,
or the fighting in our country, on our soil
with our people, will never end.

Holidaze

Trees lit, glowing with holiday cheer
then notice of a child's death
appeared on all media, the phone ringing.
The lights dimmed this Christmas Eve.

The community, school, gathered together
spoken, written, tributes, prayers for this child
battling demons, fear, too deep to face.
Where were you, we, before he took his life?

Not just this child, but countless
fighting internal, external wars
dragons of plenty, souls with unrest
unable to cope, pushed over the edge.

Why on Christmas Eve, choosing to die?
Your parents, siblings had presents for you
to unwrap. Your spirit, soul, unable to adapt
to this bizarre sentence, the human experience.

Vampires Vacuuming

We all know, felt their hoses
attaching to our necks, solar plexus.
They suck the life, our last drop out,
before we realize to shut it off.

These aren't vampires twinkling
on the big movie screens.
They take the form of mother-in-laws,
coworkers, shirt-tail relatives, "friends."

We avoid them in grocery stores
malls, most public places.
They're the reason caller ID was invented.
a Nobel Peace prize should be awarded.

These are not our good friends who need us
to listen, lend an ear, a hand, when life happens.
These are those folks who thrive in tornados
stir pots, make recipes of gossip, baking evil,

and they never, ever, stop talking.

How do we fix these modern day vampires
without smelling of garlic and Tic Tacs?
We do the best we can to be kind, considerate
making up bizarre sentences, excuses. Then

run away as quick as you can.

Twitterpated

Phone rings
heart leaps
your voice
beautiful music.

Pulses bound
breath taken
face blush
giddy excitement.

Brain disconnects
tongue ties
words form
bizarre sentences.

Holding hands
kissing lips
wrapping arms
around us.

Anxiety

Pulses bounding
sweat, an elephant
on your chest,
cloudy thoughts,
darkness hovering
instant paranoia.

Anxiety sufferers
know symptoms
never timing
causes countless
fear engulfing.

Throw quilt over
smother flames
knit, run, yoga
to reboot, reinstall
logical thinking
to heal, this
bizarre sentence.

Door Mats

I would like to think
my front door is a welcoming place,
the wreath, the mat scribed, *Welcome*,
the pots of flowers, the willow tree,
the door chimes Bach melodies.

Who comes to my front door?
I took an assessment.

My ex-monster-in-law
returned one day, she was
visiting from outer space
to beat loudly on my door.
My heart sunk into my colon.

The neighbor girls selling
those evil Girl Scout cookies.
Boy Scout popcorn, their brothers
are peddling. I hate saying no,
but it gets stuck in my teeth.

Divorce papers served, creepy meter readers,
police asking about the drug house on the corner.
Mormon children in their fancy dress,
Jehovah's Witnesses reading their devotions,
uttering soul saving bizarre sentences.

Eeeek, That's it. I am buying a new mat,
Unwelcome, Go Away, a wreath with cross bones,
new doorbell chimes, themes from *Twilight Zone*.
Unwanted visitors my willow tree will whack,
I'm painting a sign, Friends and Deliveries, go to the
back.

Food

Iced sun tea with raspberries, local honey
fills a canning jar to brim, dripping condensation.
Herbs sustained in recycled Terracotta pots.
The harvest is ready to begin.

Zucchini, deep purple, the crowning jewel
squash varieties orange, yellow, green
cucumbers, carrots, onions, berries
tomatoes every kind, even cherry.

My garden, my rainbow of life
pure energy gifted from Earth
all started from Heirloom seeds
grown with love and chem free.

What saddens me, unrests my soul
the need to make this distinction,
GMO, non-organic, preservatives, bizarre,
but money and yields became more important.

Cancer (the C word)

I wish I could write
a bizarre enough sentence
which accurately describes,
encompasses every emotion,
"You have cancer" is spoken.

Fear, to depths of the sea
to the core of the Earth, no.
Denial, anger, resentment, worry
grief, the pre-death sentence, No.
Rock bottom, twenty stories above you. NO.

There are no words, no description.
The worst word in all languages.
Why, because the word cancer
shouldn't be spoken. To speak its
name, gives it power, just like satan.

What is the key to beat this battle?
Rip it out of your psyche,
change energy to love every day,
stare fear in the face, then laugh
until this C word no longer exists.

Church Control (the other two C words)

I never understood this bizarre sentence
priest, pastors command on the altar
holding the most precious of beings
wrapped in white gowns
"You were born a sinner."

Without me standing here
dropping tap water on your head,
this cherub who traveled
from God's lap to mother's womb
suddenly became succumbed by sin? What?

The cherubs, known as babies, on Earth
bring light, hope, love, glimpses of Heaven.
Until this human man waves his cross, flicks water, this
joyous cherub is stricken by sin, headed for hell,
unless, the opportunity didn't happen, then it's Ok. What?

Heaven loves all babies. So, scare the parents a little more
if parenting wasn't scary enough. If we don't get our
child christened, a doomed life, they will surely suffer.
I, the boss man of this church, will make sure
your baby's sins are wiped clean. Here is the offering
        plate...

The God I believe in, light candles, and pray
is also in the garden, in the mall. She is with me all day.
Spirit knows the heart of every soul alive, your story,
      pain.
My God transcends the bizarre sentences scribed. The
      Sun rose
above the dogma and controlling pastors driving,
      Maseratis.

God doesn't care if you are divorced, gay, or straight
that is the church's rules, made by the state, the
      governing
body of the church, who are the most popular with the
      most money.

The church's marquee says, "We love all"(if you fit into
      our box of normal).
God, unlike church, knows each cherub, even when aged
      and raised by gays.

Gross Anatomy

Mind, body
dying spirits,
fascinates me.
Please, let me learn.

No one knows
where spirit lies
when the body
can still dance.

When spirit leaves
carcass remains.
The cells entrap
earthly demons.

I want to dig, discover
know answers
science doesn't
want to question.

I need this
to make sense of living,
studying death
and the next life.

The answers I need
lie within the simple tissues
the cells, the helix, the protons,
the samples under the microscope.

A museum of human history
the future of healing
could lie within this
cold, bizarre sentence, death.

In Limbo

Finally, I see the light.
The destination I need to travel.
The place I know I should be,
but the stars haven't perfectly aligned.

Knitting, waiting, reading, waiting, writing
working, waiting…. for the phone to ring.
Still waiting, praying, waiting, writing,
drinking tea. I can't stand this any more.

The more I reach the farther away
my dreams seem. Why can't I touch it?
What do I need to do to get there?
So much of this bizarre sentence
is out of our control. It is certainly
not from my lack of effort.

How can I chisel away at a block,
a hurdle, I can't even see?

I try to live with purpose, passion, but
with every passing second my heart sinks
further, until the day I can touch my dream
and kiss it. God, my last thread is breaking.

Oh! The phone is ringing.

Killing Game

hunted heads
sawed tusks
human hands
adrenalin rush
guns arrows
killing game
mind state
game sport
stuffed trophy
animal spirit
life lost
species extinct
for fun.

Political Sentences via Midterm Elections
(Because you can't have a book entitled, *A Bizarre Sentence,* without including something political.)

"Really?" says Michigan Republican
　Terri Lynn Land during midterm elections.
"Squeeeeel!" won gun shootin' Harley ridin'
　Joni Ernst, a seat in the Senate.

Republican Senator Mitch McConnell thinks
　he's a poet, "What rhymes with Allison Lundergan
　　　Grimes?"
Be careful Senator, for she threatens you in her TV ad,
　"Mitch, that's how you hold a gun."

Billions spent in advertising for these, brilliantly bizarre
　actual sentences, so we can know the truth,
mudslinging, during midterm elections,
　now, a note from the White House.

"Go Fuck Yourself," screams our VP Dick Cheney
　with video rolling on the senate floor.
"Facts are stupid things," Ronald Reagan admitted
　at the 1988 Republican Convention

Bill Clinton will, of course, deny all wrong doing.
   "I did not have sexual relations with that woman."
The Bush family, both Dad and Junior
   well, I don't have enough pages.

Even Jeb Bush agrees, although it's probably a ploy.
   "He resigns as George's brother"
says his aide to the New Yorker.
   I think he really wants the 2016 nomination.

We can't throw blame. We, our nation, voted them in.
   Both houses, now, are back to conservative.
David Letterman on New Year's Eve said it best,
   "The Pope is more liberal than our officials," elected.

Writing Glasses

It's a wonderful life
and a little bizarre
to own a pair of
writing glasses.

Those who do, understand,
conscious that our world
spins a bit differently,
vision obscured, acute, spectral.

Seeing the detail, smells
described, adding depth,
creating, living, loving
knowing there is only death

without the word
written, spoken,
preformed
sung, read.

Owners of writing glasses
may pen in different ways,
the essence, core of being,
a common thread, community.

Each owner of writing glasses
feels the passion, solidarity, insanity,
voices screaming in your head,
only to be bled to paper, reborn.

So if you own a pair of writing glasses,
congratulations. The word is a mighty thing.
We see and write to evolve thinking,
living in a bizarre sentence. Curse?

Free as the Whirligigs

We need to be free
from bounded roots of our past
noise in our heads
fermenting bizarre sentences.

We need to touch the fire
feel the heat, pain, sweat dripping
on our palms, neck, soul
burning passions, achieving.

We need to move easy
like cartoon shaped clouds
the leaves, whirligigs
spinning round and round

We need to see
hummingbirds, bees
feed on the exploding blooms
tasting the nectar, sweet.

We need to dance
like butterflies and dandelion seeds
relying on the breeze
taking comfort in falling free.

We, you and me, need
to be by the sea
sand between our knees
worshiping the Sun.

Acknowledgments

Books are not composed, penned, and written in a vacuum. *A Bizarre Sentence* is no exception. I would like to extend a huge hug of gratitude to:

Lori Perkins of 918*studio* press for always believing in my work and this project.

Renée Bushā of Sliced Moon Designs, thank you for your vision and expertise.

My global friends who helped me create the poem, *In Unison,* by giving me the translations in their native tongue: Arabic: Salma Arabi; Italian: Christiana Langenberg; Turkish: Esra Aiello; German: Mary Toflin; Greek Cappadocian and Modern:John Breinich; French: Rachel Brault; Persian: Shirin Hoseini.

Thank you, Ciaran O'Sullivan, for inspiring me and your pictures for *A Rubbled View* leading to the cover.

Confusion in English, the idea came from an article written by Christina Sterbenz from Business Insider Magazine, *9 Bizarre Sentences that are Perfectly Accurate.*

Biography

A Bizarre Sentence is Trisha Georgiou's fourth poetry chapbook. Trisha's works, both poetry and prose, have been published in journals including *Country Woman, Small Farm, Radish, Midwest Writing Center's blog,* and *Eastern Iowa Review,* to name a few. She is also an active volunteer and board member for the Midwest Writing Center, Davenport, Iowa.

For more information please visit her website at www.TrishaGeorgiou.com .

You may also find her on Instagram, Facebook, and Twitter.

Afterword

Georgiou has divined an uncomplicated, beautiful treatment of her subjects in *A Bizarre Sentence*. Her poetic examination is not the bloodbath of analysis or persecution, but rather a very lovely, poignant, and suggestive questioning and/or challenging on a range of aspects.

The clever usage of minimalism in poems such as *Anxiety*, *Gross Anatomy*, and *Songwriter* provide the reader with an imagist sensation and with this comes poetic acumen that packs a punch, giving us the tools to feel.

I am bounced from associations between the three C's (Cancer, Church, and Control) and moments in cafés where I sit and drink a coffee while Georgiou opens the front page headlines in the minds of coffee-drinking strangers—in this I come to understand that I'm on a journey of her consciousness. She asks me to imagine. She asks me 'why.' She asks me 'who.' An adept writer, Georgiou seeks to create symbiosis with her readers and succeeds in marvelous capacity.

Taken aback by her sharp observations—I feel that some of her panorama can scrape a reader's knees at first. Though, on the heels of that brief sting is a feeling that just around the corner are remedies of inquisitive nature. Right or wrong, she asks, but does not always stake a claim, and her poetry allows the reader a choice. In the poem *Killing Game* words like 'trophy' and 'fun' interact with 'spirit' and 'lost.' There is no tyranny of author here—perhaps a subtle inclination, but never a command.

When I read Georgiou, I can't help but to fall into the leisurely game I often play when I'm looking at the world from a fence upon which many of us teeter, wondering about the nature of both lawns below.

On her turf, she could require the reader to see only one side—hers—but thankfully she allows the humble gift of sharing perspective without creating divide.

And that is possibly the most bizarre element of *A Bizarre Sentence*—the fact that I'm allowed to be in a dreamy state of consciousness without feeling a forced opinion, a rare quality in today's poets who are intent on creating points instead of creating a feeling. In an era where brash opinion is dominant, Georgiou gives the reader an opportunity to visualize things in a free-thinking space without condemnation—a space considerate to the exploration of the matter at hand.
A chance to breathe and ponder: oh my, in these times?!
Bizarre indeed.

—Holly Norton, 2015 Midwest Writing Center
 Collins Poetry Resident